BEYOND THE
SUMMIT

ABOUT THE BOOK

Most financial advisors focus on strategies to assist you in your climb to the top—they tell you where to invest and how much to invest, they move your tools and goods around, and they make some room to play with risk. The problem is, they don't know much about strategies to assist you "after" you have reached the summit—retirement.

Changes in the condition of your life, in the lives of those around you, and in the world around you, become more pressing as you get ready to embark on "life after your working life." A successful retirement faces numerous threats: the national and global economies could tank, tax laws might change, illness could visit you or a loved one, and children or grandchildren might need college assistance—the list of "what ifs" is endless.

The View From the Summit truly takes the long view on retirement planning. On these pages you will be taken along a journey similar to that of Jeff and Kevin Buchers' clients. You will learn how the Buchers educate their clients on inflation, taxes, medical insurance, social security, and so on. You will see how they guide their clients with passion and expertise, in order to create an income plan that will protect their standard of living with certainty, while providing the flexibility needed to enjoy the desired extras.

BEYOND

THE

THE HARD-WORKING AMERICAN'S RETIREMENT GUIDE

SUMMIT

BY JEFFERY M. BUCHER *AND* KEVIN M. BUCHER

Publishing Company Name & Address:
Citizen Advisory Group
770 Commerce Drive,
Perrysburg, OH 43551

ISBNs:
978-0-692-29980-7 – paperback
978-0-692-29981-4 – eBook

Library of Congress Control Number: 2015942073

Interior design by Chad McClung

DEDICATION

To our parents who have supported and encouraged us to strive for excellence in all of our endeavors.

To our clients who have entrusted us to guide them through their retirement journey.

To the team at Citizen Advisory Group who lives our mission to serve.

To our Creator who makes all things possible.

CONTENTS

DISCLOSURE

with your financial, legal and tax professionals. Jeffery and Kevin Bucher have taken reasonable measures to ensure the accuracy of information contained herein. However, the information, graphics published may contain technical inaccuracies or typographical errors and therefore are provided "as is" without any warranty of any kind.

Investments involve risk including the potential loss of principal and unless otherwise stated, are not guaranteed. No investment strategy, such as asset allocation or diversification can guarantee a profit or protect against loss in periods of declining values. Please note that rebalancing investments may cause investors to incur transaction costs and, when rebalancing a non-retirement account, taxable events will be created that may increase your tax liability. Rebalancing a portfolio cannot assure a profit or protect against a loss in any given market environment.

Fixed annuities are long-term investment vehicles. Early withdrawal may result in tax liability, penalties and/or surrender charges. These charges may result in a loss of bonus, indexed interest and fixed interest, and a partial loss of your principal. Bonus Annuities may include annuitization requirements, lower capped returns, or other restrictions that are not included in similar annuities that don't offer a premium bonus feature. Riders are available at an additional cost and are subject to conditions, restrictions and limitations and benefits are generally not available as lump sum payout. Guarantees, if any, are backed by the financial strength and claims-paying ability of the issuing insurance company.

Reproduction, adaptation, distribution, public display, exhibition for profit is prohibited by law.

THE VIEW FROM THE SUMMIT

Imagine…you've made it!!

You worked hard your whole life. Most likely, nobody ever handed anything to you. Maybe you were the first in your family to attend college, or to achieve meaningful financial success, or both. Or maybe you come from a long line of achievers. But the main thing is, you beat the odds. You made it to the top. To the summit.

We like to compare achieving financial success with climbing Mount Everest.

That's because few people aim that high, and fewer still make it to the top. It's a steep climb, and most people turn back before the summit is even in sight.

But not you. You weathered the storms. You made a way where there wasn't a way. And you made it to the top. And the view?

Sensational.

But now what? The same way someone who summits Everest has a guide, a Sherpa, someone familiar with the terrain, you most likely had some excellent advice to get you to this point. A point at which you can retire. You get to stop climbing because, in the language of the field, you've summited.

But in our experience—and we've worked with thousands of individuals and families—there's one stark truth: Most financial advisors focus on strategies to assist you in the climb, but they don't know much about strategies to assist you *after* you have reached the summit—i.e., retirement.

Arranging for a successful retirement requires a completely different skill set. And if you thought the road to the top—the *creation* of wealth—was tricky, you should see the road back down to Base Camp.

On Everest, the downward path is steep and unforgiving, just like the real world. Instead of sudden changes in the weather like you have at the top of the mountain, you've got sudden changes in the condition of your life, and in the lives of those around you—and the world around you, for that matter.

What happens if the stock market tanks? Or the economy goes south? (Again.)

What happens if someone you love experiences a sudden serious illness or catastrophic accident? What if you need a sudden infusion of cash to pay for college for a child or grandchild, or you have some other major expense, whether expected or not? What if they change the tax code, or interest rates go up, or your healthcare suddenly doubles in price? Or some unforeseeable war or terrorist event transforms the world economy, as did 9/11?

The future is unpredictable. But the one thing we can predict with certainty is…uncertainty.

That is why we specialize in one thing and one thing alone: creating financially sound retirements for people like you—

people who've reached the summit in life and need a guide through the surprisingly perilous journey called "retirement."

The journey may not be as…well, sexy as the road to the top. Quite frankly, at this point we're more concerned with your safety than the view. We want to get you back to Base Camp. And we want to make sure that you don't run out of oxygen (i.e., money) along the way.

Most of our clients are not multi-millionaires. They've amassed considerable savings, but they're not the one-percenters. You don't read about our clients in *Fortune* and *People* magazines. But often we are able to provide them the same security and financial abundance in retirement enjoyed by people who have amassed considerably more assets than they have. In other words, we create millionaire-style retirements for people who were never millionaires. This book explains how.

This book is not for everyone. It's for those who are ready to see the view from the top of the mountain. Those who have scaled their own financial Everest—the hardworking people who made the right choices, put a few dollars aside, maybe got a little lucky along the way, and most likely had great advice about how to grow their finances. This book is about your next journey—your retirement journey. We've guided others successfully from the summit to a secure and comfortable retirement they never imagined they would be able to afford. And now it's your turn. Let's take this next phase of your life's journey…together.

WHY SHOULD RICH GUYS HAVE ALL THE FUN?

What if we were to tell you that you could live out your retirement dreams more extravagantly than you ever thought possible, without having millions socked away? What if you understood how to construct a solid retirement plan that allowed you to take advantage of the savings you worked a lifetime to build, live without the fear of running out of money, and still have money to pass on to your children?

We are investment advisors who focus on retirement strategies that give our clients confidence that they will be able to maintain their desired standard of living. We guide them through our unique retirement planning process to help them create a balanced retirement plan that allows them to be free—to go out and spend money and enjoy retirement the way they always dreamed of doing—without sacrificing the cash flow they need to meet their monthly needs. We help clients out of the vicious cycle of subjecting all of their money to the risks of the stock market and randomly taking withdrawals, hoping it all works out. With a solid retirement plan, our clients live better—before and after retirement.

Retirement has nothing to do with which stock or bond a person buys, or with what's going on with the S&P 500 or the Dow-Jones. Retirement is about golf and grandkids and travel and fun. We help clients set up a plan that will ensure their retirement includes the things that are important to them.

We take our clients through our process, which helps them realize they *do* have enough money to live out their retirement dreams. Using some of the strategies the wealthiest people in this country use when they retire, we make those strategies work for the client who wants to retire with $250,000, $500,000, or up to $2 million in investable assets. Many of our clients have been working with one of the big brand-name firms and don't understand how their portfolios work, or why they have the investments they do.

The truth is, the majority of our clients are average, hard-working American people who work a variety of blue and white-collar jobs that pay $80,000–100,000 a year. The truth is, there are many more people in this income bracket than in the $500,000 and up range.

It is our job to make it possible for people who have worked hard their whole lives to have the same quality of life in retire-ment that wealthy people have. Unlike the big, brand-name firms, we do not consider $250K, 500K, or $2 million an insubstantial amount of money. We grew up with blue-collar roots; we learned about money, and we take pride in the impact we've made when a retiree leaves our first meeting saying, "I didn't know I could do that. I never understood how my money was working until today."

Our planning process can completely change the course of our clients' lives by showing them how to go live the retirement they always thought was meant for someone else. Sure, our process could also change a $10 million retiree's life, but doesn't he have enough choices already? If he could leave his $10 million in a money market account and make 1.5 percent and live to 95 and be fine—isn't our time and expertise better spent helping the more typical retiree make a plan? We are here to offer the rich retiree's plan to the regular retiree.

When a client walks through our doors, they are not "regular"; they are not just a number or a portfolio to us. During our very first meeting, we strive to treat our clients better than any other financial planner ever has. When people trust their money to big, brand-name firms, they are often made to feel like their $400,000 isn't "good enough," because the majority of the firm's other clients have a lot more money than they do. But our clients know that we understand and respect how hard they have worked and how well they have done. We also understand that when it comes to retirement planning, the stakes for our clients differ from the stakes for the ultra-wealthy.

The moment we sit down with a new client, we begin clarifying what they want their retirement journey to look like so we can determine what investment tools they will need. We explain the concepts of their finances to them in ways they can actually understand—leaving the tricky language to other advisors. We work together to create an income plan that will protect their standard of living while providing the flexibility they need to enjoy the desired extras and handle emergencies as they occur (this plan also includes strategies to deal with inflation and taxes). Finally, we educate our clients about medical insurance, and assist them in evaluating their short-term and long-term insurance options.

After our clients have left our office, we communicate with them regularly and continue to educate them. Our clients can expect to receive weekly e-mails and quarterly newsletters. Twice a year, we conduct in-person State of the Market addresses, at which we bring our clients up to speed on the latest market news and trends, and explain how these changes relate to their portfolios and their retirements. We know that during the course of our clients' retirement journeys, there will be market fluctuations and regulation changes. We are committed to keeping our clients abreast of all news that pertains to their retirement plans so that we can explain it, and keep fear at bay.

Because of the way we are compensated, our clients' success—the success of their portfolios—is linked to our success,. As a fee-based advisor, the balance of our clients' accounts is just as important to us as it is to them. In 2008 the market went down 37 percent, and our accounts went down 37 percent—which meant we took a 37 percent pay cut. Most big, brand-name advisors get paid up-front commissions, meaning there is less incentive to care about what happens to a client's money after it is invested. Sometimes the market takes a turn for the worse (as it did in 2008), and if clients panic enough over losses or potential losses, the big, brand-name advisor gets them to make changes—which leads to buying new stuff, and he makes more commissions. Just as the $10 million dollar retiree's stakes are lower than the everyday retiree's, the brand-name advisors suffer less than we do when clients' portfolios suffer. When we say, "We are in this together," we mean it.

By providing our clients with a high-level understanding of how their money works, and how to invest it with an eye toward the retirement journey they want, we are able to figure out the specific details that need to go into their plan. Our typical client is so pleased by her newfound understanding of these concepts that she doesn't need to know all the details—she trusts us.

One reason it is difficult to build trust when it comes to retirement planning is that approximately 90 percent of Americans do not understand how the investments they have accumulated will relate to their lifestyle after retirement. How do you translate the money in your portfolio into travel, golfing, and leaving money to your children?

Our approach is to invest in financial tools that provide predictable cash flow to meet monthly needs, because everyone understands how the difference between $5,000 a month and $8,000 a month will affect their lifestyle. By presenting money to our clients in a clear and digestible way, we eliminate much of the guesswork. Whereas other advisors may benefit from keeping their clients in the dark—by keeping their money tied up for potential growth—we encourage our clients to get a solid grasp on the various types of funds they have, so that their lives and dreams grow.

If you listen to what Wall Street has told you your entire life, you might believe earning and saving money is all about accumulating wealth and growing a nest egg. But sadly, if your retirement is approaching and you don't have enough saved, the remainder of your working life becomes a race against time. Adding insult to injury, if you end up running out of money, your advisor on Wall Street—and the whole system—points a finger at you and says, "Shame on you. You should have saved more."

Rejecting Wall Street's marketing scheme, we suggest that instead of growing a nest egg by trying to accumulate as much as possible, our clients allow us to help them figure out how to replicate the golden goose of their job so that it can lay eggs for them throughout the rest of their lives. We encourage clients to forget what they have been led to believe—that it is all about accumulating some magical amount for retirement, and that they have to invest in the stock market for growth in order to increase that magical number. We remind our clients that if they put all their eggs in one basket, what they are ultimately doing is increasing risk to their retirement. Wall Street is encouraging people to take their nest eggs and set them outside in the unpredictable storm of the stock market. Retirees cannot rely on that strategy to provide them comfort in retirement.

Our planning process is unique. Many people are being underserved by the big brokerage firms, and we want to reach out to these people and say, "Why are you allowing your advisor to take your money and place it in a bunch of investments without explaining any financial concepts or providing any underlying reasons for the choices he or she has made?" Advisors in the big-name firms have been trained to sell securities. We have nothing against them, but they're investors. We are planners.

People should go to investors if they have some extra money they want to figure out how to invest. People should come to us if they want a plan for their retirement. We understand that many people take pride in going with a big, brand-name firm, but the reality is they are not getting the best service because the big, brand-name firms are too busy servicing their high-end accounts.

The everyday American retiree is *our* high-end account. We put as much thought into serving our $250K retiree as we do our $2 million dollar retiree. Trust us when we say that catering to the $10 million dollar man is not our goal. Clients who come to us can trust that they are getting a complete plan, as well as the same Ritz Carlton service the ultra-wealthy demand.

Wall Street's plan is to show people a Monte Carlo simulation: they will say, "If you invest your money here, you have an 87 percent chance of making it. Those are great odds, and this is a great portfolio." We ask our clients, "And what if, as you were boarding an airplane, you were told you had an 87 percent chance of making it to your destination? Would you stay on that plane?"

The reality is, without a true plan, 90 percent of people are on that plane as they head for retirement. We are telling people—Disembark! As leaders in the area of high-level retirement planning for the mainstream American family, it is our duty to ensure that all our clients reach their destinations.

2

THE RETIREMENT JOURNEY: WHAT TO EXPECT ALONG THE WAY

Ninety percent of the population simply has investments. As they head into retirement or begin retirement planning, they hope things will work out. But because they are living on hope, they often either overspend or underspend. They end up losing control of their finances in their golden years, and thus cannot relax the way they always dreamed they would be able to.

We show our clients how to plan for retirement *knowing*, not hoping. Our clients do not have to study finance or interest rates or the S&P 500 to understand the big picture. They do not have to concern themselves daily with the ticker on Wall Street. They do not panic when the market dips, and they do not go on spending sprees when the market rises. We give our clients the essential retirement planning tools and maintain open lines of communication from day one.

The first and most critical step toward building a successful retirement plan is the first meeting, which many of our clients tell us is unlike anything they have ever experienced. Most advisors start the first meeting talking about investments and rates of return. What we talk about is The Journey. When new clients walk into their offices, most advisors hand them their bags—already packed. These advisors have this good investment and that great one, and *voilà*—the client's portfolio is ready to go. These advisors never even bother asking their clients, "Where do you want to go on The Journey? What do you want it to look like? What will you need to get there?" In our office, those are three of the most important questions we can ask. Once we understand what kind of retirement journey our clients want to take, we know how to pack their bags with the appropriate financial products.

We liken retirement assets to a diamond: At the top of the diamond is the total amount of retirement assets—let's say $100,000. From the top of the diamond, going down either side, we allot these assets into safe products on one side and riskier products on the other—in this case $50,000 in safe, $50,000 in risk. Where the diamond comes back together at the bottom is their income. The diamond concept gives clients a rough idea of how much money they can draw every month to live on.

Our ultimate goal in running this safe-to-risk assessment is to get to the bottom of that diamond and create a Written Income Plan—your spending plan. Our Written Income Plan helps clients lay out their expectations for the rest of their lives, and it helps them concretize and ultimately realize The Journey.

It involves conducting a complete analysis of the various ways they can draw upon their Social Security, and finding them the best option. If a client has a pension plan, we add it to this Social Security foundation and call this Protected Income. If we layer in an annuity, the annuity will have a guarantee of income as well. We encourage clients to keep some of their money in protected places—for example, in savings and checking accounts at FDIC insured banks, in CDs, and in fixed and fixed-index annuities.

The Written Income Plan breaks the retirement income sources into two categories: Protected/Structured Income and Variable/Flexible Income. The Protected/Structured Income comes from a source that provides some type of guarantee and is safe regardless of what happens in the stock market or how long a client lives. It will provide a fixed structured payment that may adjust upward to assist with inflation. An example of this is Social Security—which provides monthly payments that are guaranteed by the U.S. government and include cost-of-living adjustments. Variable/Flexible Income is income at risk—which doesn't mean it is not safe, but simply that it is unprotected or not guaranteed. An example of this type of income would be a client's stock market accounts.

With this income, we assume a sustainable withdrawal rate, just as other advisors do. The big difference is that other advisors assume these variable rates on a client's entire portfolio, while we build in guarantees to cover the basic living expenses needed to maintain a client's lifestyle. We look at the financial products as building blocks. Our view is that a good balance can be reached that maximizes the advantages and minimizes the disadvantages of each financial product, and blends them, so that in the end our clients walk away with a solid, properly constructed retirement plan. For us, the investments that make up a client's portfolio are not the solution—the investments are simply tools and parts of the plan. The plan is the solution.

When clients work with us to create a Written Income Plan, they gain certainty—they know that they will have X dollars coming in every month after retirement. The stock market will do what it always does, but even if it disappears like the dinosaurs did, the client's Protected Income is still there.

The stock market, of course, will likely never disappear... and neither will inflation. The Written Income Plan takes inflation into account. If a client's stated retirement goal is $50,000 a year, in twenty-five or thirty-five years he is going to need twice that amount per year. Seeing the impact that even a modest 2 percent inflation rate can have over a twenty- to thirty-year retirement period can be a shock. Strategies to deal with inflation are a critical component of our clients' plans.

Our clients often see for the very first time a Written Income Plan. The Written Income Plan shows how much income they can expect and rely on in retirement—the protected income. For the first time they can see actual numbers and can ask themselves, "Okay, can I live off that?" Taking those initial steps is a very powerful and empowering process for our clients.

Once we have a client on board, we begin tax reviews. We evaluate different tax strategies that help clients minimize their current and future tax liabilities, because the reality is that most of our clients' money is likely tied up in qualified plans—like IRAs or 401(k)s—and the tax has never been paid. Through no fault of their own, most people have no plan for taxes—most people are just going to take the money out and their CPA is going to add it up—and taxes are one of the biggest expenses these people will have in retirement.

So wouldn't it be wiser to be forward-thinking? Yes. Wall Street wants people to think successful retirement all comes down to the accumulation of more and more eggs, but they neglect to address the biggest expense retirees are going to have—taxes. Who cares how much more money someone has made if they have to pay an outrageous percentage of it back in taxes? When we ask clients if they were comfortable with the way their former advisor went through their tax return and helped them determine how to work their portfolio so that they could reduce their tax bill, most of them say, "My advisor has never looked at my tax return."

We look at our clients' tax returns and help them figure out how to take advantage of the tax code. Working with us, clients learn how to get money out efficiently with the least amount of taxes due. They leave our office with a plan for withdrawal, so that they pay as little tax as possible for the remainder of their lives.

As we mentioned, we see retirement as a journey, and along any journey, we need to protect ourselves from bandits that come our way. One of the biggest bandits is taxes—and the other big bandit is health.

We help protect our clients' retirement money from the

costs of short-term and long-term illness by educating them on the complex subject of health insurance. We assist our clients in evaluating the insurance options available and make sure they have the coverage they need at the best possible price. We cannot stress often enough the importance of having the appropriate health care plan in place, and in Chapter Eight we cover more thoroughly just how costly having the wrong plan can be in terms of money and a family's well-being.

Most advisors talk to clients about how to grow their accounts, take the income they want, and figure out how to ensure that there is plenty left over for their kids. But what happens when a client's concerns about their legacy bite into their journey, their life after retirement? What if our client has constructed a legacy on purpose, meaning they took out a life insurance policy guaranteeing that upon their death a set amount of money would go to their children?

To sum up, we look at our clients' money, separate risk from safe so that a portion of that money is protected from the stock market, and build an income plan to make sure they have enough money to live on for the rest of their lives, allowing for inflation. We address health and life insurance concerns—setting up a life insurance plan that allows a client to pass money on to their children, tax-free. Again, clients who come to us after working with other advisors often have never been told that passing on other types of investments—such as 401ks—often results in their children having to pay high taxes and fees—meaning they do not get the amount of money the departed intended to leave them.

One of our biggest aims is to encourage our clients not just to get their hard-earned money to their children tax-free though life insurance, but to spend their money now—during their lives and in their retirement. If we set up the appropriate Written Income Plan, our clients will not need to worry if their accounts dwindle over the course of their lifetimes. By creating a legacy on purpose, they ensure that it doesn't matter if they have $1 million today and $300,000 when they pass away, because their children will be guaranteed a set amount, not just whatever is left over. A well-planned legacy protects not only the client's lifestyle, but their children's inheritance also.

From day one with our clients, we dig deep to understand The Journey they desire. We assess where they keep their money and how they will access it. The goal with retirement planning is never to hoard that $1 million a client has worked so tirelessly for. With a properly constructed plan, you can comfortably spend down your assets throughout your retirement, secure in the knowledge that the income necessary to maintain your desired lifestyle is protected for the rest of your life—and the legacy you intend to leave for your loved ones is insured.

Wealthy people look at the common people and say, "Gosh, they're taking all the risk and paying all the fees." And when the results are bad, your advisor says, "Gosh, we couldn't have predicted this. We're so sorry." The reality is that most people have the resources they need to take control of their financial futures. Just this year, we established a Written Income Plan for a recently remarried widow. She and her new spouse each have roughly $1 million. This woman has been saving her whole life to pass money on to her children, afraid to spend any of that $1 million on herself.

In our first meeting, it was clear she was very risk-averse. We were able to create a Written Income Plan that included enough Protected/Structured Income—guaranteed to last the rest of her life—that she was able to create a legacy of $1 million, on purpose. She did this using only a small portion of her assets, and now she knows her kids are going to get $1 million, even if she spends all of the $1 million she has squirreled away for sixty years.

What did the creation of a Written Income Plan result in for this woman? Last month, she took thirty-two family members for a one-week vacation at one of the nicest resorts in the mountains of Virginia—something she had never thought possible. The bill was probably $30,000, and she used that money to *live* and create lasting memories—which we believe constitute a true legacy. We love to hear such stories from our clients. The whole point of earning and saving money is not to hoard it or run the risk of losing it due to stock market losses, but to use it for yourself and for the people and the things that you love.

SAFE MONEY, THE CASH YOU CAN COUNT ON

In this chapter, we are going to address safe money. We believe in the power of the stock market and in the value of having investments in the stock market, but we also believe that as our clients approach retirement, time is no longer their friend—and safe investments are a must. Clients can expect to discuss proportion when they come to us: What portion of your assets is safe, and what portion is at risk? These numbers should then make sense in consideration of two factors: Your risk tolerance, and the income needed from your retirement assets to meet your monthly needs. Over a thirty-year or forty-year period, the stock market is likely to perform very well, but our clients do not have decades to ride out the fluctuations. They need access to the money they have saved right now, and that is why some of this money has to be protected.

Some of our clients come to us with a portfolio that con-

sists of almost no risk, and others come to us with way too
much risk. Very few people are where they need to be, right
in the middle. We explain to the client who despises risk how,
by sticking completely to safe investments, they will lose purchasing power because of inflation. More often, of course, we
see people who are taking on far too much risk. These people
know from past market experience that their financial picture
is skewed, but they don't know how to fix it. They don't want
what happened to them before to happen again, but they don't
know where to turn. Their current advisor isn't offering them
any new solutions that would address their uneasiness, but we
are able to show them—for the first time—alternative solutions
that provide the answers they have been looking for.

If a client's portfolio is extremely safe, they will lose the
battle with inflation. By contrast, the client who comes in
after having been sold a bill of goods by Wall Street worries
that they now carry way too much risk relative to their age,
temperament, and needs. In either case, our goal is to talk
common sense. There is a balance every client can and should
maintain between money that is safe and money that is at risk,
and we show them how.

Most advisors believe there is safe money and risk money,
but differ in their definition of *safe*. For us, *safe* means principal protected—meaning that portion of a client's money is
not affected by what happens in the market. It is completely
principal-protected by whoever is offering the guarantee—for
example, an insurance company or a bank. To say that money
is at risk does not necessarily mean it is risky—it just means it

THE CASH YOU CAN COUNT ON

is not safe; it is not principal protected. The best illustration of the value of safety is this: when the market crashed in 2008, the portion of our clients' money that was in safe investments did not lose a dime.

Another value of a safe investment, which we will explore in later chapters, is that many types of safe investments come with a degree of income guarantee. As our clients get closer to retirement, not only do they have to protect what they have saved over the course of their lives, but they also need to have a plan for getting their money out of those investments. Safe investments make it clear and simple.

There are five basic principal-protected investments:

Insured deposits, such as banking accounts

Certificates of deposit (CDs)

U.S. federal savings bonds

Fixed annuities

Fixed indexed annuities

Clients may not value the low returns on their savings or checking accounts, but money in the bank is safe, necessary, liquid, and accessible. Money in the bank is insured by the bank, and if the bank has a problem, FDIC insurance backs it up. It is important to maintain a reserve fund in the bank—emergency cash—so that if something goes wrong, you can easily get to your money. We advise our clients to keep anywhere from three to six months' salary in savings. But again, just as every client has a personal preference on the proportion of safe to risk money, every client should pick a dollar amount for their emergency fund that makes them feel comfortable.

Another safe place for clients' money is in traditional fixed annuities and fixed-indexed annuities. When a client's money is in fixed annuities, it is protected should the market stumble. Fixed annuities and fixed-indexed annuities are investments made with an insurance company, as opposed to a bank. The insurance company guarantees that money, and just as the FDIC backs up the banks, if the insurance company experiences trouble, something known as the state guarantee fund steps in and guarantees a client's money up to state guarantee limits.

When clients come to us and ask, "What's in an annuity for me in terms of safety and value?" we first explain that double-layer system of guarantees. We then explain the difference between a traditional fixed annuity and a fixed-indexed annuity. A traditional fixed annuity has contractually guaranteed rates of return as far as the interest that will be credited. Just like with a CD, when clients invest in fixed annuities, they will know the interest rate. It could be an adjustable interest rate, or it could be a multi-year guaranteed fixed rate.

The fixed-indexed annuity also has an underlying minimum guarantee of interest, but it has upside potential based on the performance of a stock index—typically the S&P 500. Clients choose fixed-indexed annuities because they have decided to take on some risk pertaining to how much interest they will gain by accepting a lower guarantee in exchange for the possibility of earning more. Still, fixed-indexed annuities are principal protected, and thus safe from stock-market losses.

Annuities make sense for retirees because they are the only financial product in the universe that can provide a lifetime of guaranteed income. Clients who come to us are sometimes concerned about the costs of annuities, but we explain to them the many different types of annuities and the varying cost structures available. The actual client fee for a fixed annuity or a fixed-indexed annuity is very low, as opposed to a variable annuity that is in the market—variable annuities typically carry significant fees.

Another common misconception clients have before meeting with us is that if they put their money into an annuity, either they will lose all control of their money or it will be locked up and they will be unable to access it. Typically, however, an annuity provides 10 percent access per year without penalty. Indeed, liquidity is a concern for retirees and people coming into retirement, but it is for this very reason that we advise our clients to diversify—our clients do not put all of their money in annuities.

Clients also mistakenly believe that investing in annuities means that should they pass away prematurely, their heirs will not see the money. Again, we walk clients through the various types of annuities and the various kinds of things these annuities can provide. Annuities are not only backed by insurance companies, but in many types of annuities, the client retains control of the lump sum, and upon death, the beneficiary inherits the balance of the account.

Another important benefit of the fixed and fixed indexed annuities is the automatic capturing of each year's returns. Each interest credit that is applied is locked in and not at risk to be lost due to poor stock market performance. On the other hand, when investments are exposed to the stock market's volatility, several years' worth of positive returns could be wiped away with one stock market downturn. The only way to capture the return in these risk investments is to sell them at the right time, a difficult process to manage. Capturing your gains is critical to the long-term success of your retirement plan, and with the fixed and fixed indexed annuity products this happens systematically, without having to sell.

CDs offer the same advantages and disadvantages as fixed annuities—except that they can't provide a lifetime income guarantee. Our clients also worry about the lack of liquidity that comes with CDs, but on balance, they find it reassuring to have some of their money in a safe place. As with a fixed annuity, a CD is offered for a specified number of years at a specified interest rate, for example, three years at three percent, or five years at five percent. Historically, fixed annuities have paid a tad better than CDs, and the interest on annuities is tax-deferred, so clients don't pay any interest until their money is withdrawn from the account.

The final protected investment is U.S. Savings Bonds, which are guaranteed by the U.S. government. U.S. Savings Bonds are sold by agents authorized by the Treasury Department. Interest earned on U.S. Savings Bonds is exempt from all state and local income taxes, but the investor must pay federal income tax on the bond at the time of maturity.

For clients who are averse to playing it "too safe," we ask, "What kind of loss did you experience in 2008?" The common answer is 30 percent. If a client lost 30 percent on $1 million, they lost roughly $300,000. We then ask, "How would you feel if that happened to you again?" Finally, we show clients how if they invest 50 percent safely and 50 percent in the market—or whatever ratio they choose—the next time the market crashes, they will lose 30 percent only on their risk investments. Their aggregate total loss will be only 15 percent, and minimizing downside losses is critical to retirement success.

We always tell clients that no matter how they proportion their safe-to-risk investments, and no matter which types of safe investments they choose, they have to be careful. Many clients come to us when they realize that their advisor has only sold them fixed annuities—because some cannot sell anything else—and that having all their eggs in one basket is not working well for them. It does not work well for anybody. Some advisors try to make certain products look like the answer for retirement, but products or investments are never the answer—they are tools with which to build your Plan.

Many of these tools sound good to our clients, and we often hear, "Do I need all these tools? A mix? How will you help me determine what goes into the mix?" At this point, we look at how much income our clients need in order to maintain their lifestyle, how much reserve they have—on-hand immediately—and that combination of factors determines the mix.

Investment products and their terms will change with time, but our strategy will not, nor will the outcomes we are trying to achieve with our strategy. Our strategy works at all levels of income. The less money a client has—obviously—the less they will have for retirement, but we have found that an adequate retirement is entirely possible for people who have saved $200,000. Whatever lifestyles our clients are leading, the money they have saved is enough to make this system work—and work very well.

Our work begins the moment our clients answer our first question: What do you want your retirement journey to look like? We seek a balance—no overspending, no underspending; no all-safe, no all-risk. The balance we achieve is always personal—and ultimately it comes down to how much a client is willing to risk. Most of the people we work with do not want to risk much.

There is an age-old rule that all financial planners cite at some point: the Rule of 100. It suggests that investors subtract their age from 100 to determine how much of their money they should put at risk. An investor's age indicates how much money he or she should harbor in safe investments—so the sixty-year old investor should have 60 percent of his or her money in safe investments, with 40 percent to risk. Most financial planners agree with this rule in theory, but differ in what they consider to be safe investments. Of course, the Rule of 100 does not suit all of our clients. In the next chapter, we will talk about different types of risk-bearing investments—and how they are a necessary piece of every retiree's puzzle.

RISK-BEARING INVESTMENTS: HOW MUCH SHOULD YOU HAVE IN THE MARKET?

One of the most dismaying statements we hear from the people who come to us for help is, "I'm not surprised I was receiving such poor service from my previous advisor, but I didn't know there was an alternative." The first thing we say to these clients is, "You aren't alone."

The majority of Americans have been conditioned to accept the Wall Street approach to portfolio building and customer service. We are conditioned to believe our broker may not call us back, and conditioned to believe our broker when he tells us, "Don't worry; you've lost money, but everyone has. It's okay." Over time, the American investor has been conditioned to believe market losses are "just paper losses."

Wall Street's marketing forces reign supreme, but investors are tired of being patted on the head and told, "Sorry, we could not have predicted that downturn." From day one, we tell our clients they deserve better treatment and better answers, because they have worked hard for their money. When we sit with them and review their safe money versus their risk-bearing investments, we explain what carrying too much risk in their retirement portfolio means as they actually draw nearer to retirement. And when we explain how and why they got to such a risk-heavy place, many of our clients realize for the first time that their brand-name investment-house broker has been not been acting in their best interest, but in his own.

We believe in investing in the stock market, but we have found that many of the clients who come to us for help are taking on far more risk than necessary for the retirement journey they want. We find a frightening number of people investing the same way they did when they were younger and retirement was in the distant future. These people, who are now closer to retiring or are already retired, cannot sustain the losses they could when they had sufficient time before retirement to recoup them. Financial losses are never fun, but at least when people are young there is time—and despite losses, they are depositing a portion of their paycheck into their portfolio and buying when the market is down. "There comes a point," we tell our clients, "when you can no longer afford to lose money."

We advise our clients to take on the smallest possible amount of risk while still achieving the returns that will allow them to reach their retirement journey goals. We do not look to Wall Street as a model, but to large academic institutions like Harvard and Yale. We figure there are some pretty smart people at those universities, so we ask ourselves, "How do Harvard and Yale manage their endowments? How can we apply what they do with their $60 billion portfolios to our clients' $60,000 portfolios?" The large academic institutions diversify their portfolios among a variety of asset classes around the world. In addition to the standard mix of stocks and bonds, they include alternative investments like commodities, precious metals, and real estate, thereby limiting their risk and downward pressure if the market collapses. We figure if what the academics are doing results in success, we will mimic their processes and choices and achieve the same results.

Our clients understand immediately that our first priority is ensuring that their portfolio choices do not put their lifestyles at risk. We put the necessary amount of money in safe investments to protect that lifestyle, regardless of market performance, and put the rest in risk-bearing investments. We do believe in the long-term power of the stock market, but our clients leave our office knowing that the money they will rely on every month will be safe, and it will not be affected by market fluctuations. The most crucial factor in constructing their risk-bearing portfolio, we explain, is diversification. And then we explain the difference between *true diversification* and the type of diversification Wall Street has conditioned Americans to trust in.

In 2008, the common investor believed she possessed a diverse portfolio, and was then shocked at her losses. The problem was that brand-name advisors had assured their thousands of clients that diversification simply meant having a mix of stocks, equities and bonds, and fixed income. The typical Wall Street brand portfolio contains mostly U.S. stocks and bonds, with a small amount of international stock mixed in for good measure. This approach has proven to provide little true diversification, as U.S. stocks and bonds have grown more and more correlated. The problem with this definition of diversification, research suggests, is that investments move as an asset class. This means that owning stock in IBM, Apple, or McDonalds might matter in the short term, but over the long haul, it is more important to have some money invested in the top U.S. companies, but to have other money invested in other asset classes.

We truly diversify. Our clients' risk-bearing investments include big and little U.S. companies; stocks and bonds; U.S. and foreign investments; silver and gold; commodities such as cotton, coffee, corn, and wheat; and master-limited partnerships—which are oil- and transportation-related investments. For clients who have never heard of some of these investment classes, or who never realized these types of investments were an option for them, we explain that over the past decade, these were some of the top-performing assets, and they are now easier than ever for the investor to attain.

By spreading our clients' money across a broader spectrum of asset classes, we significantly reduce risk. When one asset class fumbles, the other takes up the slack—and vice versa. The traditional U.S. portfolio failed in 2008 because the traditional U.S. investor listened to the traditional Wall Street spiel. The traditional U.S. investor who was headed toward retirement listened to the traditional broker, whose job it was to sell the securities he had on his shelf. The traditional investor may not realize that the traditional broker receives incentives to sell certain mutual funds—i.e., to sell certain products and investments that the company owns and wants to get rid of.

We are completely independent, and we tell our clients, "With us, there is no conflict of interest." We do not have products we need to sell on our shelves—we have nothing on our shelves. Once our client has told us the type of retirement journey she wants to have, we go out into the open marketplace and design her portfolio based on research and on her needs. As we mentioned in an earlier chapter and will probably mention again, because of the way we are licensed and paid, our financial well-being depends on the financial health of our clients' portfolios. Wall Street brokers, on the other hand, do not typically get paid unless they make changes to portfolios. They typically make a living based on transactions, not on the performance of their clients' portfolios. Once you have completed your transaction, their incentive to provide service and add value is gone unless they can convince you that another transaction is necessary.

Wall Street has done a great job of making it difficult for the consumer—the investor—to muddle through the process of truly diversifying a portfolio. Clients have been conditioned *not* to ask, "Is the advice I'm receiving in my best interest, or am I receiving this advice because it is in the best interest of my broker, or the company he represents?"

The typical broker is a registered representative of his or her company, and therefore represents the company and the company's interests, not the client and his or her interests. By contrast, we have fiduciary duty to our clients. We work in our clients' best interest, we disclose fees upfront, and we disclose conflicts of interest. As investment advisor representatives, we are advisors, and when a client hires us, we work for her, not for a firm.

It is the Wall Street broker's job to make "suitable" recommendations to their clients, but in our book, "suitable" constitutes the lowest standard of care. The problem is, *suitable* can mean anything to anybody, and Wall Street plays on this. If our clients tell us, "We're hungry," we could offer them a candy bar. A candy bar is suitable. Filet mignon is also suitable. We can satisfy our clients' hunger—our clients' needs—with chocolate or with steak. Unlike other brokers, however, we point out to clients the differences in suitable caloric intake, suitable nutritional value, and suitable cost structures—for that particular client and their lifestyle. When our clients are better informed, they are better satisfied.

The brand-name brokerage-house brokers get compensated if they sell their clients something. When discussing how to invest clients' money, these brokers do what they need to do to meet the lowest standard of "suitability" and to fatten their paychecks. We, on the other hand, are not compensated up front when our clients make their investment choices. Our compensation depends on the value of our clients' accounts, which is based on how well their portfolios are performing.

Now that we have raised skepticism about Wall Street's policies and processes, how can we expect people who are planning their retirement to trust that we are different? A simple Google search exposes thousands of companies that make this claim.

If investors believe their advisor can do all the research, make all the security selections, manage market fluctuations, reduce their tax bills, plan their legacy, protect them from health care issues, and juggle hundreds of clients at once—they are being fleeced. If the same people in charge of planning your financial future are also investing your money—we smell a rat. We know we cannot effectively manage our process for all of our clients alone, and for this reason—we outsource part of the job to professional money managers whose sole task in life is to invest our clients' hard-earned money.

The people we hire to make securities selections and manage our clients' stock market investments are experienced and qualified. Unlike typical brand-name brokers, who mainly receive sales training, our money managers receive financial strategy training, focusing on retirement planning that results in optimal client outcomes. Our money managers are not trained to sell IRAs, but to maximize IRA performance.

Our money managers share our philosophy that our clients' lifestyles should be protected with non-stock-market products. There is a place for risk in every portfolio, but we do not find it practical to put a client's lifestyle at risk. By relying too often on the stock market to produce reliable income during retirement, Wall Street types are willing to risk all of a client's money— because it makes *them* money. The client ends up taking all the risks, paying all the fees, and hoping for the best. Clients who are stuck in the Wall Street mentality need to ask themselves what we encourage all our clients to ask themselves: "Am I willing to sacrifice my money for my broker's lifestyle?"

Again, we look where Wall Street does not look. A recent Harvard study posed the question, "Why does an investor get the returns he or she gets? What are the determining factors?" Researchers found that 93 percent of an investor's return was based on which asset classes the investor owned. Only 4 percent of a return was dependent upon which particular individual securities were selected, and 3 percent was dependent on timing. We believe—and our money managers believe—that the goal of retirement portfolio construction should be for our clients to own the appropriate mix of asset classes based on their individual risk profile. Too many advisors spend time on what to buy and when; we believe in managing asset classes because they tend, on the whole, to move together.

Similarly, the way we invest in the stock market differs greatly from the way the brand-name firms invest. We invest institutionally, meaning we group everybody with the same risk tolerance, life goals, and timeframes into the same portfolio—that is, how clients' investments are broken down into safe money versus risk money, and which investments they own, is identical for people with identical lifestyle parameters.

The brand-name broker builds a client's portfolio based on what the client wants, but also maybe based on who the broker ate lunch with yesterday and who is offering a sales bonus that month. With this broker, two couples walk in just months apart and find they have two entirely different portfolios. "Well," says the common investor, "Isn't that good? Aren't we all unique? Shouldn't we get a unique portfolio?"

Our answer is a definitive No. Investors often do not get calls from their brokers, not because the broker does not care, but because the broker has no idea what his three hundred clients own—they all have unique portfolios. How can these brokers possibly manage these portfolios, and more important, how can they steer their clients away from risk?

We are different. If there is a problem, our money managers know it and they know how to fix it. Our clients do not have to call us—we call them. From the first meeting onward, we see ourselves as navigators on the ship of our client's life journey. We will not board a sinking ship, and we will not let our clients take certain risks.

YOUR INCOME PLAN...
AND DON'T FORGET INFLATION

People who come to us, whether they are in retirement or about to retire, usually ask four questions:

Do I have enough money for retirement?

What is retirement going to look like?

How much can I spend?

Is my money going to last my lifetime?

We tell them, "Let's put some numbers down on paper,"
and we create for them a Written Income Plan.

Most of our clients have never seen a Written Income Plan.
Most of their advisors have never taken the time to sit with them
and do the math that is required to optimize their retirement
monies. Most advisors know how to sell investments, but do
not have the expertise to pull all the pieces together to build a
reliable plan. Clients whose advisors have been working as their
investment manager, sales person, and planner find themselves
scratching their heads and living on hope and hypotheticals.

And then they come to us. We take the time to do the math and pull the pieces together. Furthermore, we outsource to our expert money managers so that when it comes to retirement planning, we can offer service that nobody else can.

Almost 100 percent of the people who come to us are winging it in terms of how they are living off their portfolios. Either they come to us too scared to spend (thus cheating themselves out of the retirement they envisioned and deserve) or they have already begun to overspend, and are living in fear that they will soon run out of money. The root of their problem is that they were conditioned to believe the Wall Street way was the only way—but they have come to realize that all the pretty charts and all the focus on building a nest egg do not translate well into a consistent, sustainable, monthly income.

For too long, most American investors have focused on getting to the top of the mountain, but have forgotten the most essential part of the trek—getting back down off that mountain safely. Going up a mountain without a plan is like going into retirement without a plan. Wall Street has persuaded people that the goal is getting to the top—that is, reaching that magic retirement number—but in reality, reaching the peak is only half the battle, and the advisors who assisted their clients on the ascent may not be the best advisors for the descent.

We like to celebrate our clients having made it to the top of the mountain— we know that saving their hard-earned money all those years was no easy task. But we also know that a higher percentage of deaths on Mount Everest occur on the way down the mountain than occur on the way up, and we know that almost 100 percent of the time, people come to us because they feel suddenly stranded—their advisors have said, "You made it. Now, best of luck getting to the bottom." Their advisors leave them with no map for the trek down the mountain because with their approach, the final destination was the top of the mountain.

We explain to our clients that the guides who took them to the top do not have the relevant experience and expertise we do to get them safely off the mountain and back to Base Camp. In reality, the descent—the path to a safe retirement—is more dangerous and rigorous than the climb up. Once a client has reached Wall Street's magical number of eggs in the nest, it is no time to take huge risks. None of our hard-working clients got to the top by taking huge risks; they were prudent, they took measured steps, and they rationed their supplies.

Our clients have a great advantage, because when they come to us, they receive a Written Income Plan. Their energy on the way up may have been focused on touching the summit—the top value of their money—but on the way down their energy is focused on the top value of their life, the goal being a safe return to a great retirement.

Most people come to us with a basic understanding of their income needs. They are fifty or sixty years old, and they know what they need to live on. Whatever the number is, we work with our clients to create a Written Income Plan that will guarantee they their desired level of income will be protected—no matter what conditions the market throws at them—for the rest of their lives after retirement.

We start by separating clients' essential needs from their "fun stuff." Essential needs usually include housing, cars, food, and medicine, and we ensure that these needs will be met on the safe income side—through social security, pension, and annuities. Safe-side income is not only guaranteed, but usually provides Cost of Living Allowances (COLA), which automatically take inflation into account. On the fun side, we invest in risk-bearing assets—diversifying these assets, of course, as we noted in the last chapter. We also make sure some of the monies on the risk-bearing side are in investments that react favorably to inflation, such as commodities, metals, and certain types of bonds like treasury-inflated protected securities. And always, we like to remind our clients that just because some of their "fun side" investments include the word "risk," this does not mean these investments are risky—there are many levels of risk-bearing accounts

Typically, people come to us with no plan for income. Sure, they have the nest egg, but they pull from that nest egg without a plan, and without realizing—because before meeting us, nobody ever told them—that they could be living a less fearful, more fulfilling retirement if they concentrated more on their income plan. Even when clients know about the 4 percent withdrawal rule (which will be covered later in this chapter), they do not always know what amount of income they can take out. They come to us confused and sometimes fearful. We assure them it is not their fault. Wall Street has made them believe it is all about the nest egg, about reaching that magical number and making it to the top of that mountain. "But," we ask them,

"What if your nest egg was $0 and you were living off $50,000 a month income. Would you care about that nest egg?"

Most people answer "No." And when they express concern about leaving money to their children, we say, "We also have better ways of dealing with that." We will get to these solutions in later chapters.

Our unique planning process doesn't discount the value that a nice nest egg provides when it comes to flexibility and discretionary spending. For this reason, our approach is to sacrifice as little of your nest egg as possible to achieve the financial security that a protected income stream provides. Just as having the right mix of safe and risk assets is critical, so is having the right mix of protected income and a nest egg.

What it comes down to for our clients is the need to know they will have enough, rather than hoping they will have enough. When they tell us they need $6,000 a month to live on, we add up how much their social security will provide when combined with their pension and annuities. This is mathematically guaranteed income, and it is safe no matter what happens to the market. Many people, after seeing their first Written Income Plan, realize they have saved enough money to have an even better lifestyle in retirement than they had hoped for. Putting their numbers on paper not only provides a mathematical guarantee, but psychological relief. Clients leave our office feeling secure and free

Our Written Income Plans are custom made according to our clients' needs—but our process is the same for everyone. We ask all of our clients the same questions, beginning with the essential: What do you want your retirement journey to look like? As we have said, that is when we go about the business of packing their bags with the things they will need. We go through their safe and risk investments and discuss inflation. If they need $6,000 in monthly income now, we explain that they will need twice that amount in twenty-five years, due to inflation.

Most clients understand inflation, and in fact, many have been told by previous advisors that they must take it into account. The problem is, advisors with a strict stock-market orientation use inflation fears to convince consumers that they need to stay in the market with all of their savings and continue to risk their financial futures. They have been advised to simply continue to grow their money, and that the only way to do that is by taking risks. Make money, save money, take risks, buy and sell stocks—if these clients feel they are racing against time before retirement, the pressure will be tenfold after they *do* retire!

The problem is, what works in the accumulation phase does not always work in the distribution phase—and we are experts in the distribution phase. We build sustainable Written Income Plans, emphasizing that retirement is not all about the nest egg. We emphasize the journey and the mountain. While we certainly take into account all the financial challenges our clients have faced and conquered by making it to "the top of the mountain," we focus much more on getting them safely back to Base Camp—happy retirement.

Going up the mountain, issues such as inflation and market

volatility can be annoying. These issues can make a client's journey more challenging, but they do not really matter. On the way down the mountain, on the last steps home, these issues are *all* that matter, and their effects can be devastating. These issues can force retirees to spend less, or to migrate back into the workplace. We create Written Income Plans so that our clients never find themselves having to scramble to fix things after it is too late.

It is true that studies have found we spend less as we age— we eat out less, we travel closer to home, we do not have to own the latest in fashion or gadgetry—and so some of the purchasing power we will lose due to inflation is offset. Still, we maintain our stance with our clients, advising them to ignore the Wall Street philosophy that in order to keep up with inflation, they must make risky investments. If people are invested too heavily on the risk side of their income plan when the market takes a hit, they experience a double whammy—inflation plus their market losses. We have found that the best way to deal with inflation is not to lose money.

Wall Street has always issued safe withdrawal rates—it used to be 8 percent, then it was 6 percent, and now it is 4 percent. Some studies say 4 percent is too high. So what is the retiree to do? We ask clients, "Are you willing to get to the end of your life and not have any income?" We say, "As you descend that mountain toward your goal—toward your dream retire-ment—how well-equipped are you, and how will you handle your journey if conditions suddenly change?"

Conditions will change, and life will throw curveballs,

but with a Written Income Plan, our clients worry a lot less than they used to—and they will worry less when a crisis does hit. We know of married couples who have no idea what will happen after one of them dies. And while this conversation is never a comfortable one, the reality is that one half of a couple will always die first, and that is when the true value of having a plan will become most apparent.

"When one spouse dies," we ask, "how much income will be lost? How will the surviving spouse replace it? Will he or she even need to replace it?" Most people are conditioned to say, "We would rather not have this conversation, and will deal with the loss and loss of income when it happens." We offer this: There is a safer, smarter way, and its payoff will go beyond finances— the payoff will be peace of mind. Maximizing Social Security survivor benefits and having adequate life insurance coverage are usually more attractive solutions to our clients than simply setting money aside—money that they could be enjoying now. Again, planning ahead reduces the stresses that are specific to retirement years by ensuring that when a beloved spouse dies, a financial cushion is there to make the fall bearable.

Throughout the income planning process, we take a client's evolving needs and feedback into account—if and when life throws a curveball, or when a client has special needs, we react with creative solutions. Throughout our relationships with our clients, we advise them to follow the age-old financial wisdom of staying the course—that is, we advise them to stay the course we have provided them with, because it is a good one, created with their best interests and best retirement journey in mind.

SOCIAL SECURITY:
WHAT YOU DON'T KNOW CAN HURT YOU

For many people, Social Security is the foundation of their retirement income—and often it is the largest source of that income. There are many ways to collect Social Security benefits, but most people make collection decisions without even being aware of these different ways. Or they spend too little time analyzing their options, not thinking about the long-term effects of shortsighted decisions.

Obviously, bad decisions regarding Social Security can be catastrophic to retirement planning; at the very least, they can result in people not living out the retirement they had hoped for. When people come to us, they often hear for the very first time what options are available to them for collecting Social Security. Our clients learn that they have been considering Social Security in its narrowest terms, and that we can provide new information to them so that they can make smarter decisions.

The first step anybody has to take in retirement planning is to sit down with an advisor—like us—so that we can explain the available options. When clients meet with us, we give them the necessary tools to analyze their choices regarding Social Security. Our tools are easy to understand—we use software that analyzes our clients' options and presents it to them clearly on a spreadsheet. If a client chooses Option A for drawing on Social Security, investing a certain percentage in this annuity and that stock, their monthly income is Result A; if a client chooses Option B, with different strategies toward Social Security and so on, their monthly income is Result B—so we are able to provide a side-by-side comparison of all the different choices our clients want to consider.

Our mantra about Social Security is "Don't let it just happen." Most people assume Social Security is a given, with no alternative ways of maximizing its benefits. They make uninformed decisions about when and how they should file. Because Social Security is such a complex monster, we understand how people are in the dark about how to make these decisions. But retirees who don't know all the rules of the retirement game—just like baseball players who don't know all the rules of baseball—are playing at a severe disadvantage.

Social Security is a hedge against longevity, because it is one of the few sources of income that is guaranteed for life. It also comes with cost-of-living adjustments (COLA) and step-ups to the surviving spouse, so that there is some survivor protection. As valuable as Social Security is for protecting oneself and one's spouse against those key risks—longevity, inflation, and survivor income—it is still a topic that most consumers and advisors have very little knowledge of. All most people know about their Social Security benefits is what they see on their Social Security statement, which says: "This is your retirement benefit at age 62, at age 66, and at age 70." Because the Social Security Office is not allowed to give people advice on filing strategies, the public is mostly unfamiliar with the other benefits they are eligible for, and how or when they can be used to increase their Social Security benefits. There are retirement benefits, spousal benefits, and survivor benefits. Even people who are currently single may be eligible for those spousal and survivor benefits if they were once married. The Social Security Office calculates what an individual's benefit will be, but if the individual does not ask the right questions, they will not get the right information.

The right information—the information our clients come to learn about—helps them form the whole picture. The puzzle pieces are:

The client's retirement benefit
The client's spouse's retirement benefit
What the client is entitled to as a spouse
The client's longevity
The client's other retirement assets
The client's retirement income needs.

All of these pieces go together to determine the right Social Security claiming or filing strategy.

Social Security is a retirement benefit, but this does not mean an individual has to collect it immediately upon retirement. It may be in the client's best interest to use some of their other retirement assets, allowing their Social Security to accrue interest. By waiting, you are eligible for a larger monthly benefit, and this larger monthly benefit will be with you for the rest of your life. Our approach is to figure out strategies that will provide our clients with their maximum possible Social Security benefit without significantly affecting their other retirement assets. Coordinating your Social Security filing strategically with your other retirement assets is critical, as the short-term and long-term effects on your portfolio have to be evaluated.

Let's consider the case of John and Jane Doe. Jane Doe, age 62, has filed for her Social Security Benefit and is collecting $1,230 per month. John Doe, age 66, has not filed for his Social Security benefit and is attempting to determine when would be the best time for him to do so. According to John's Social Security estimates, he could collect $1,800 per month if he started his benefit now, at age 66. On the other hand, if he chose to wait until age 70, his estimated monthly benefit would increase to $2,376 per month. This is the basic information that most people consider when making their claiming decisions. However, there is another element that should be factored into the decision that most people are simply unaware of: because John Doe has reached his Social Security Full Retirement Age (age 66), he has the option to file a Restricted Application for a Spousal Benefit. This allows John to collect a Social Security Spousal Benefit based on Jane's earnings history. The spousal benefit is 50 percent of Jane's Full Retirement Age benefit amount, even though Jane began receiving her benefits at age 62, prior to her Social Security Full Retirement Age. By filing the Restricted Application for Spousal Benefit only, John will begin collecting $820 (50 percent of Jane's Full Retirement Age Benefit amount) per month at age 66 while still earning the 8 percent Delayed Retirement Credits on his own Retirement Benefit, which he can switch to at age 70 ($2,376 per month). During this four-year span, John will collect nearly $40,000 in Social Security Spousal Benefits that he, like most people, was completely unaware were available to him. This illustrates that the decisions about Social Security are not just about when you should file, but also about *how* you should file. Being informed about your Social Security filing options is critical to making a decision that will meet your goals and objectives.

Another client we are working with is a sixty-six year-old-woman who is now single but was married for nineteen years when she was younger. This woman didn't realize that she was eligible to collect a benefit off of her ex-spouse. She thought her Social Security benefit was only connected to what she herself had earned, but we showed her that she can collect a benefit from her ex-husband's Social Security that is equal to what she can collect on her own record. So instead of filing for her retirement benefit, she's filing for her spousal benefit, and that allows her to earn the 8% delayed retirement credits on her record and to switch to her own record at the age of seventy—with a pay increase from Social Security that will last the rest of her life. She will earn thirty-two percent more at the age of seventy than what she is collecting today because she's using what we call "the switch strategy."

The Social Security administration would never write an

individual a letter suggesting they file for spousal benefits only and then switch to their own record later, but Americans have the legal right to do so, and we have the software that enables us to present these calculations to our clients.

The earliest an individual can file for Social Security collection is age sixty-two, and 42 percent of the population files at this age. By doing so, they are taking the lowest benefit amount possible. Of course, some people do this out of necessity, but more often than not, they do it because they have never been told they don't have to, or that it might be in their best interest—literally and figuratively—to wait.

Decisions about Social Security are a function of a client's total income plan—the monthly dollar amount they will need, and when they will need it. After we narrow those two things down—how much money and how often—we build an optimized plan to include our clients' Social Security on the safe-income side, along with annuity payments and pensions. We run those numbers beside their risk investments and build a cohesive plan.

People who opt not to take advantage of the Social Security piece of their retirement plan are essentially opting to lose thousands of dollars. We do the analysis for our clients—we do it all—in order to get the most out of the Social Security system. Social Security for many couples is a $1 million asset in retirement—that is, it *can* be a $1 million asset for people who plan properly. Knowledge is power, but when it comes to Social Security planning, knowledge is also actual money.

Again, Social Security statements—and even the benefit

estimator calculator on the Social Security Administration's website—only calculate an individual's retirement benefits. The system itself will never explain how couples and divorced or widowed individuals can maximize what they could receive over their lifetime.

Knowledge is power—knowledge is actual money—but if people don't know what they don't know, they may not even understand that they should be looking for this information. Sixty percent of our clients are seeing for the very first time the extra thousands of dollars in retirement income they could collect. Forty percent of our clients are somewhat familiar with their Social Security options, but they don't understand the fine print because there are so many rules and so many unique situations. There are literally hundreds of different ways for a married couple to collect Social Security. Our software can run through these options in a matter of minutes. Our spreadsheets illustrate to clients how their informed choices now will affect their retirement numbers later.

Across the political spectrum, there are fears about the government's Social Security commitments in the coming years, and we address these issues with our clients. In our opinion, the current concerns over the future of Social Security are not going to have an effect on our clients who are fifty-five and older. There have been two changes to Social Security throughout its history, and both have included some form of grandfathering protection for those who are already receiving Social Security or who are nearing retirement age. Even if the government eventually makes drastic changes to the system to solve its problems, it will be years before those changes are implemented. We stay abreast of current research and recommendations, and we keep our clients informed about how potential changes might affect them.

One final thing to mention about Social Security benefits is that they are built with cost of living adjustments (COLA). While it is likely that how COLA is calculated will change in the future, it is currently based on the recipient's initial benefit base. This means that someone who files at age sixty-two instead of waiting and filing later will get lower cost-of-living adjustments for their whole life, because COLA adjustments do not compound.

The Social Security benefits an individual is entitled to are based on the rules of the system, and an individual who knows the rules of that system can take better advantage of it. The Social Security statement isn't going to clarify the rules for anybody, and the calculator on the average advisor's website isn't going to help the client understand those rules, either.

We have become expert in this subject because it is important to our clients' retirement options, and because it is our mission and our passion to provide our clients with the retirement journey they've always hoped for. Social Security decisions are million-dollar decisions for most people, and if we are going to set them on the retirement journey they have always dreamt of, we had better take our time and understand the complexities of Social Security benefits and collection.

7

TAXES: KEEPING MORE FOR YOU, GIVING LESS TO THE GOVERNMENT

Taxes are among the major expenses for most retirees, but most people have no plan for how they are going to attack their taxes so as to minimize their payments to Uncle Sam throughout their lives. Helping our clients create an income plan includes helping them build a strategy for taxes.

We have worked with Ed Slot, whom the *Wall Street Journal* calls one of America's top IRA experts. He points out that when most people think of their IRA or 401(k) or 403(b)—or any type of retirement account—they think of the number on their statement—but in fact, that balance is not their money. The day an individual opens a 401(k), he or she goes into partnership with Uncle Sam—and the day that individual wants to pull money out of the account, Uncle Sam asks for his share. "What is your plan," we ask our clients, "to ensure that you're going to get the lion's share of that account and pay the least amount possible to Uncle Sam?"

For most people, there is no plan. Most people are just going to go through life and take their random withdrawals—and they're going to pay the tax. We urge our clients to be more proactive than that. During the first part of our review process, we go over our clients' tax returns to determine where their income and taxable liabilities come from. Second, we arrange their investments in different ways in order to reduce their tax bill. Moving forward, we look to see, as clients begin to pull money out, if there are strategic ways they can make these withdrawals—again, the goal being to pay the least amount of tax over their lifetime.

Say for example, we found that a client had a high amount of taxable interest; for most people this isn't the case, because interest rates are very low in today's market. But if a client does have a high amount of taxable interest, an annuity could be a very smart place to transfer some of that money because annuities are tax-deferred. Let's say this client has a CD that's making interest; we could take that CD and put it into a fixed annuity—which will work almost identically to the CD, except the guarantee on the money is issued by an insurance company instead of a bank. By putting that money into an annuity, interest is tax-deferred. It will not show up on a client's tax return, and it will immediately reduce their tax burden.

Let's look at another case, taking a business owner, John Doe, who had a large medical expense last year, and thus a tremendous number of deductions. Mr. Doe may be in a fantastic position to Roth convert, meaning because his income was low—because of deductions or business losses, or for whatever reasons—he could pull money from his IRA and convert it to a Roth IRA, which would result in either no tax or very little tax. Too often, people believe their accountant is going to help them manage their taxes, but in reality, most accountants only add up the damage—damage which in many cases results from the poor choices an individual makes with his or her financial advisor.

Because we know that most advisors do not look at their clients' tax returns or ask their clients certain types of questions, when people come to us for the first time they may learn that they have—thus far—missed a few golden opportunities, and once certain opportunities are gone, they never come back. This is why it is so important for retirees (or those nearing retirement) to know what their advisor is doing to manage their tax burden. What continuing education conferences are they participating in to stay on top of the tax codes, to understand changes, and to learn the different types of strategies regarding IRAs? Advisors and accountants have to work together to make sure their clients pay the least amount of tax possible upon retirement and throughout retirement. We build strong ties with accountants and continue our education in order to stay abreast of tax law and tax changes, and this enables us to reduce our clients' tax bills by as much as 20 to 30 percent.

We sometimes manage our clients' taxes with a strategy we call "bumping the bracket." In 2012, the 15 percent tax bracket was $70,700 for a married couple, meaning they could make up to $70,700 and would pay 15 percent tax on that upper income. We recommend to our clients who make

$60,700 (just $10,000 beneath the 15 percent tax bracket) that they "bump the bracket," meaning they take $10,000 out of their IRA and convert it to a Roth IRA. Why? Because we know what today's tax bill will be, as opposed to what it will be if we put that bill off until later, when tax rates will likely be higher. So why not pay the 15 percent rate and have that $10,000 in a tax-free account for you and your heirs, should they inherit those funds? This strategy would also reduce future IRS-forced distributions for those above the age of 70 ½, and could potentially reduce the amount of tax you pay on Social Security benefits.

The opposite scenario would be one in which the couple does not take that $10,000 out, it ends up growing, tax rates go up, and they end up paying more tax on more money. We recommend getting the $10,000 out sooner rather than later, while we know what the tax rates are—because they are likely to be lower now than they will be later—and we can convert it to something that is going to be tax-free for the rest of their lives. Most advisors—again, just like with Social Security—don't suggest these conversions because they figure there is nothing in it for them; they don't make a dollar. It is work, but if by doing that bit of work we enable our clients to have a better retirement journey and pay less in taxes over their lifetime, we have done our job.

It doesn't matter if a client has $10,000 to Roth convert, or $2,000—it just makes sense to seize opportunity when it comes knocking, and get that money to a place where it can grow tax-free for the rest of the client's life. And then, when it is time to use that stash for income, it is still tax-free. A Roth conversion involves taking any IRA accounts a client owns and transferring some or all of the money into a Roth IRA.

It is important to understand that a Roth IRA is not an investment vehicle—it can be anything from a savings account and a CD to a stock, bond, or mutual fund. The Roth IRA designation is applied in terms of the investment's tax status. When a client converts an IRA to a Roth IRA, they have to pay the tax that year. So if our couple above, who are in the fifteen percent tax bracket, converts their $10,000 to bump the bracket, they will pay the federal government $1,500 the year they make the conversion. The advantage is that $10,000 account is now tax free for the rest of their lives, and if they pass away, their kids will inherit that account, which will hopefully consist of both principal and growth. As long as our couple has the money to pay that tax and is staying within the same tax bracket, it makes sense to take advantage of the tax bracket they are in, in each given year.

On the opposite side of that, especially for people under 70, at age 70 ½, IRA rules require that they pull their money out and pay taxes on it. If a client does not have a plan and just waits for that time, they are most likely going to have more money—and will pay a higher percentage of taxes. The man without a plan pays more taxes on more money.

The rules say that the very first time you open a Roth IRA account, you cannot pull out the interest without paying an IRS penalty of 10 percent for five years. A lot of people think they understand that penalty, and they think it sounds drastic.

But let's look at our $10,000 couple again, and imagine that in year two they need $5,000 and want to pull money out. They can pull $5,000 out of that Roth IRA and not pay a penalty because they are taking out their principal, not the interest—the interest comes out last. So the five-year rule that most people hear in regards to Roth IRAs very rarely impacts them, because it only comes into play if they cash in the entire sum.

Other strategies for reducing taxes during one's lifetime—holding off for now the question of reducing taxes upon passing—include optimizing Social Security and controlling dividends and interest in non-qualified or non-IRA accounts. Ultimately, these strategies require our clients to meet with us for an annual review so that we can explain to them any tax law changes and differences in new investments. In these annual meetings, we bring clients up to date on all the information they need to make the best decisions. Of course, we are always available to discuss our clients' concerns at any other time of the year.

We do the work the average advisor does not do. We help make sure our clients are getting the appropriate deductions in terms of healthcare and long-term care insurance—which in some cases are deductible. Clients who give charitably (as the rule stands at the time this book goes to print) could qualify for certain deductions if the gift comes directly from their IRA. Finally, our advisor fee can potentially be deducted from our clients' taxes.

We are not accountants, and we advise our clients to discuss all tax questions with their tax advisors and with their accountants. We do work with our clients' accountants, discussing what we are doing in terms of our clients' portfolios and verifying the results our software helps us generate. For instance, on the Roth conversion, we'll run a sample "What If?" tax return through our software with the new numbers, and we'll analyze how any adjustments will affect a client's taxes. Again, that's another service most advisors do not provide, and if there is even the slightest doubt, we consult with tax experts.

Indeed, there are accountants who go beyond the call of duty, but for the most part people go to their accountants with a stack of W-2s and 1099s and say, "I need to get my taxes done by April 15th. Here." But unless they see something glaringly obvious, that tax preparer or accountant for the most part is simply entering numbers into their software program and letting the tax return work itself out. While the accountant is looking backwards and giving people their tax return from last year, we are looking ahead and dealing with the long term. We sit with our clients and say, "Let's look at this year. What can we do this year to reduce your taxes? What can we do this year to reduce your future taxes? What could we do for the next five years to reduce your taxes?" These meetings make a big, big difference.

Most accountants—and in particular most tax preparers—are trained to do one thing: try to keep your tax burden as low as possible on a past-year basis. They are not planning; they are not forward-thinking. In their minds, they question why anybody would pay tax now when they could defer it until later. But the reality is, the more you defer, the more you build what Ed Slot calls "a tax time bomb." You have to have a plan. And to stress the urgency of building a plan, this is what we tell our clients: Think of the tax-planning portion of your Written Income Plan as a game. In the first half of the game, your team goes out and completely dominates, running the score up so that at halftime, you are so far ahead that you don't even go out for the second half. In the second half, though, the IRS cleans your clock—because you stopped playing. In an earlier chapter, we referred to climbing Mt. Everest, emphasizing the very same idea: the second part of the climb—or the game—is as important as the first.

Most people just have an advisor invest their money, with no plan, and their bags are packed before they even walk through that advisor's office door. But we roll up our sleeves and figure out what our clients want their retirement journeys to look like. We look at the bandits that will come in the way of our clients' retirement goals. One bandit is taxes. The other is the client's passing, which we will discuss in Chapter Nine.

What it comes down to is that we not only plan our clients' taxes now, but also after their passing. With most advisors, the entire conversation revolves around which investments to buy and when to buy them. Readers of this book, like our clients, now understand that this is secondary to understanding the retirement journey they want to take—investing is secondary to laying out the steps that will bring their dreams to fruition. We write up an income plan, and we factor in taxes because it doesn't matter how big a client's income is if half of it goes to the government. We build plans that allow our clients to live out their retirements with certainty rather than hope, and to leave legacies to their kids.

PROTECTING YOUR HEALTH ALONG WITH YOUR WEALTH

As we write these words, the process of implementing the Affordable Care Act—aka Obamacare—has begun. The Exchange has been established, and the rules are being worked out. Obviously, this constitutes a major change in health care in the United States, but we typically get involved with our clients' healthcare issues when they are 65 and on Medicare, so we won't be addressing Obamacare in depth because it does not affect most of our clients.

Once Americans get to the Medicare stage of their lives, there are basically two kinds of people: those who have employer-based healthcare coverage, and those who do not. For clients who have employer-based healthcare coverage, their previous employer is going to handle their health care and they probably aren't going to need to do much on their own. Still, erring on the side of caution, we do suggest our clients evaluate what their former employer's plan offers and compare it to what is being offered in the private market in order to determine if the plan they have is of good value. Clients without employer coverage, who are on their own for healthcare coverage in retirement, are eligible for Medicare at 65.

Medicare benefits comprise two parts, hospitalization and doctoring, which cover a good chunk of an individual's healthcare needs. However, because of gaps in coverage, many people opt to take out other types of policies. Medigap policies, by supplementing Medicare, cover the majority of gaps within the Medicare program. The value of any Medigap plan is that subscribers have very little to no out-of-pocket expenses for health care, depending upon which of the standardized Medigap plans they choose—but they do pay a premium. We ask our clients if they are willing to pay a premium, and find out how they can reduce their premium.

Many companies offer Medigap plans, and because we are an independent company, we can talk to our clients about the range of options out there in the marketplace. These options allow us to ensure our clients will have the least expensive plan for their needs. People who are on an inappropriate or unnecessary type of plan are wasting thousands of dollars a year, which in retirement can cause significant financial worry.

As an alternative to Medigap plans, there are Medicare Advantage plans. With Medicare Advantage plans, individuals opt out of Medicare-provided benefits and choose benefits offered through a private insurance company. A private insurance company becomes their sole provider for healthcare insurance. Insurance carriers offering Medicare Advantage plans are subsidized by the government-run Medicare program. These plans typically will come with a network of doctors and hospitals a subscriber can use, and there are co-pays and deductibles. Individuals choosing Medicare Advantage plans usually are choosing a plan that offers lower monthly premiums in exchange for potential higher out-of-pocket expenses.

It is important for people making healthcare and Medicare decisions—even if they are past age 65 and already on Medicare—to review their healthcare plans, because there are frequent changes in the benefits and provider networks. Every year, we sit with our clients and look for opportunities for them to lower their premiums or obtain better or different benefits. It is of tremendous value to our clients to be able to come to our office for a complete analysis of all the available plans and all the different ways they can elect to get their healthcare coverage.

For example, there are many options for prescription drug coverage, and each one is going to have its own formulary (formularies are the prescriptions covered by an individual's plan). This means different co-pay structures for prescriptions—for generics, the brand names, specialty drugs, and so on. There will also be different pharmacy networks where people can get their prescriptions filled.

These prescription plans are annual contracts, meaning there are annual adjustments to their co-pay structure, formularies, and pharmacy networks. By reviewing these changes with us, our clients sometimes discover that the lowest-cost premium plan they have been on for years is ending up costing them thousands of dollars out-of pocket per year because their plan doesn't cover their prescriptions, or the co-pay is outrageous. We utilize Medicare's online Plan Finder to conduct an analysis of all the plans that are available. We are then able to present our client with a comparison of costs—the premium, the co-pay, the money they have been throwing away—so that we can formulate the best strategy for their healthcare costs after retirement.

Most advisors don't even get into the subject of health care because it is not a high profit-margin product. But we say, "Health care and taxes are the two largest expenses our clients will face, and we would like to help manage those expenses." We incorporate health care into our clients' Written Income Plan because it has a profound impact on their retirement journey, from a protection standpoint and from an expense standpoint.

Prior to becoming financial consultants, we worked selling health insurance, and we all too frequently saw people who didn't have a plan for their retirement—and many of them were completely at risk. At that point, we decided to build a new company, and to align ourselves with financial and retirement experts so that we could help people not only with their Medicare insurance, but with their finances as well. We offer the complete package. Most advisors don't strategize as we do because they don't want to deal with the complexity and yearly changes associated with health care. Because we got our start in heath care, and because of the way we have set up our firm, we are able to provide one-of-a-kind expertise, and we employ certified Medicare experts on our team.

We want to make sure that none of our clients go through what we have seen happen to some people. We all know smart people who have been successful business owners for much of their lives, who have become powerful and wealthy—and yet, they didn't really take care of their health, so at an early age, they suffered a stroke, a heart attack, or some other type of serious health crisis. One stroke, or one car accident, can lead to several surgeries, and then ultimately perhaps to home health care, which is a significant drain on financial assets.

If our clients have the right insurance coverage in place it can provide many benefits for their families, no matter how many surgeries they need or what their ongoing health care costs. First and foremost, the appropriate health care insurance protects assets, meaning ultimately that our clients' families remain loved ones and not caregivers. With the proper coverage, our clients can get proper care so that their relationships stay intact, and so do their assets. No one should ever have to go broke due to a healthcare situation.

Clearly, there is short-term health care and long-term health care—and the latter is any type of extended health care situation that follows you around like a cloud for the rest of your life. Statistics tell us that one out of two individuals will need some sort of extended care at some point in their life. When most people hear the words "extended care," they think of a nursing home, but the reality is there are many different types and levels of care—assisted living, home health care, adult daycare, and so on. We say to our clients, "That cloud will follow you. You can buy an umbrella, or not. But if you buy the umbrella, you can be confident that you will be able to get proper health care whenever you need it."

We are always strategizing so that our clients live *knowing*, and not *hoping*. Without that umbrella, they'll spend their retirement days worrying about storms. With the umbrella, they won't need a spouse or a sibling or a grown child to leave the job market to become their caregiver. We feel strongly about purchasing long-term care insurance so that if and when something happens to our clients—or our own family members—they will be able to receive the proper care without sending family members into turmoil.

There are different ways to ensure that long-term care expenses are covered. The traditional method involves paying a monthly or annual premium for some sort of benefit. If you don't need care during your life, you lose all the money you put in. This type of long-term health insurance is similar to car insurance—we pay for it and hope we never have to use it. If the money goes down the drain, we accept that fact; but if we need that money for health care, we are thankful.

Asset-based long-term care is different—subscribers use their assets to get benefits—and there are two types of this kind of insurance. The easier of the two types of plans to understand is the annuity type asset-based long-term care plan. With this plan, if a client puts $100,000 into an annuity, the annuity grows interest, and the client can take money out if they need it—for whatever purpose. However, if this client needs to withdraw funds for long-term care, that annuity will provide as much as triple its value in long-term care benefits—an annuity that was originally worth $100,000 now is valued at $300,000 in benefits available for long-term care. We recommend this to clients who do not like the idea of paying a monthly premium for coverage they may never need; this annuity is there for their long-term care if they need it, and the funds are accessible should they decide to use them for something else. If they should pass away and never use it, their beneficiaries receive the annuity's full value.

The challenge to acquiring long-term care insurance is qualification—it is the hardest insurance to qualify for from a health standpoint. Typically, these plans are underwritten in a manner that allows the company to look at an individual's health history and determine whether they're willing to give this particular individual insurance or not. Because the risk is so high for long-term care, the underwriting is stricter than with any other type of insurance. We bring this up with clients because sometimes people think it's fine to hold off: "Oh, let's just wait until we're a little older and closer to needing care." The problem with that strategy is that none of us knows when we might need care, and if the unexpected occurs earlier in life rather than later, we may find ourselves not qualifying for the insurance coverage we need.

Getting our clients to spend money on care insurance can be a challenge—the biggest obstacle being the belief that they won't need it. We hear this all the time—"Declining health? It's not going to happen to me." And we hear, "Wow, it's very expensive and I may not need it." To that we say, "Yes, it is expensive, but not nearly as expensive as long-term care will be if you need it. And if you need care, not having this kind of insurance might wipe out all of your assets."

In today's marketplace, there are very solid plans offered by very solid insurance companies. For clients who can afford it, we say, "Pay the premium, buy the umbrella." Part of the retirement journey is money and part is living as stress-free as possible. Clearly the math is crucial (and we always look at it), but so is the emotional side of retirement. You can worry the rest of your life about the financial impact a health care issue would have on you and your family, or you can buy a good policy and make the cost of necessary health care the least of your concerns. With good short- and long-term care health insurance, you can ensure that in the event of disease or illness, all your energies go toward healing, getting healthy, and living the best life possible—financial worries will not drain you.

For many people, the cost of an annual premium is probably about one percent of a portfolio, so if they can use one percent of their portfolio to protect the other 99 percent, why wouldn't they? Some of our clients can afford to plunk down $100,000 on an annuity and pay off their long-term care right now; some of our clients go the traditional route and pay a monthly or annual premium. The key is that either route can enable our clients to live out a platinum retirement.

We assure our clients it's not a question of whether to take the family to Disneyland or buy long-term care—they can do both. Money isn't the issue; the issue is getting our clients to recognize the need for long-term care, even if it means driving home the point with a question like, "Why should that guy's mother be taken care of and not yours? Why should your adult children worry about becoming caretakers—becoming part of the "sandwich generation[1]"—while that guy's children have no such concerns?" Long-term health insurance is not just about the money—it is ultimately also a way to protect your legacy, a subject we will cover in more detail in the next chapter.

It is very important for people to see that long-term care is not just about going to a nursing home and giving up their freedom. There are many forms of long-term care, and having a long-term care insurance policy frees you. Studies have shown that having the appropriate coverage keeps you out of the nursing home and independent for longer. We tell our clients that the optimum time to purchase their long-term healthcare plan is usually between the ages of 55 to 65, and we suggest they buy it for themselves and for their spouse.

The whole idea of retirement is not to worry about the financial markets, and not to worry about all the what-ifs regarding health and health care. Our role is to manage risk so that our clients can go off and play. We work with our clients on their health care options because health care is the number-one risk to their financial portfolio. If people don't plan properly for health insurance, the results can be catastrophic, even if they have made all the right financial decisions outside of health care.

1   The term *sandwich generation*, coined in 1961 by writer Dorothy A. Miller, refers to a generation of people who care for their aging parents while supporting their own children.

Our passion is to assist people in living out the retirement journey they have always dreamed of, which involves more than just money. The biggest risk to our clients' finances is their health, and we can help manage that risk by guiding them to the appropriate insurance programs in order to minimize concerns about the cost of necessary care. We want our clients out there living their lives to the fullest. We aren't here just to sell our clients a bunch of stocks and bonds and mutual funds, only to watch them go broke because we didn't protect the most precious resource they have: their health.

YOUR FINANCIAL LEGACY, HOW TO LIVE AND GIVE THE WAY YOU WANT TO

Creating a purposeful legacy entails retirement planning that goes beyond growing your accounts. From the get-go, one of our mantras to our clients is: We will help you prepare a purposeful legacy to guarantee that your children and grandchildren will get the money you want them to have—without cramping your style.

Naturally, everyone has different goals in retirement. Some people want to spend all of their money—they feel that they've earned it, so they're going to spend it. On the opposite end of the spectrum, there are people who don't spend a dime because they want to leave as much money as possible to their family. The majority of people fall somewhere in between, but no matter what, if part of a client's goal is to provide a legacy for their family, we find them the most financially sound way to do so.

When we hear a client say, "Oh, leaving money to my kids is not important," we know that what often underlies this statement is fear. The reality is, as people begin to near retirement—as we age—we begin to worry: "I'm worried about getting myself through life. I can't worry about my children—who are grown adults." What it all comes down to for us, then, is setting up an income plan. When we set up a plan that shows our clients how income will be generated for them and for their spouses for the rest of their lives, no matter how long they live, it empowers them to see things differently. It empowers them to give while they are alive, and to leave a legacy through life insurance, because if the income is there, they see that they may as well spend it. Our income plan allows many clients to spend while they are living and still have money to pass on to their loved ones when the time comes.

Working with us, our clients begin to see their money as more than just stocks, bonds, and mutual funds. They see at it as a tool to be used to benefit themselves and the people and causes they love. Our clients plan for their legacies to go not only to their families, but to organizations and charities as well. A local man who passed away recently gave a million dollars to our city's park system. That gift will significantly benefit many families in our community for decades to come—and the truth is, many of our clients discover they too can make this type of impact if they plan properly.

Our planning process involves first understanding our clients' expenses and income needs. Many people's portfolios generate more income than they need to live. Most advisors say, "Take that excess, reinvest it, and grow it—for your future and for your kids' futures." What we say differs. We assure our clients that if they have a solid income plan that uses both safe strategies and risk strategies—if there is a high level of safe-side income—then they can rest assured that every single year that income will come, and they can be comfortable spending it. We suggest to our clients that they spend that income while they are living, either on themselves, their children and grandchildren, and their favorite charities, or to leverage those extra dollars with life insurance. Most people do some combination of all these things.

When our clients make the shift from living their retirement on confidence rather than on hope, they spend a little more. They take bigger vacations, and give some money to their kids while they are young and building their own families. At the same time they are spending more on travel and grandkids, our clients are also taking some of that income each year and putting it into life insurance—which allows them to continue to pass money on to their kids after death. Life insurance is the best way to guarantee tax-free death benefits.

Let's imagine a client with a $500,000 portfolio. We will build an income plan that shows this client he can have the yearly income he needs. He will have the discretionary funds he needs for the extras in life, and for emergencies as they occur, and he will have a $500,000 life insurance policy. We call this "portfolio replacement life insurance," because we are replacing the client's portfolio with life insurance. If he has $500,000, we're taking $500,000 of life insurance out, which allows him to go out and spend every last dollar without worrying about running out of the income he needs to live. This empowers him to do things he never thought he could do, whereas if he followed a typical advisor's advice, this same client would be hoarding his money, reinvesting, and growing it in an account. Most advisors tell their clients to hold money in an account because the more money there is in the account, the more money they—the advisors—make.

At this point we want to reemphasize that all of the pieces of retirement planning fit together and are dependent on each other. If we set our client up with an income plan, a legacy plan, and life insurance, but we don't provide for long-term health care—everything is out the window the moment that client falls ill. Without the sort of long-term care plan we addressed in Chapter Eight, if a client needs to go into a nursing home and has to use all of his money to pay for care, the entire plan blows up.

One of the fears many people have when shopping for life insurance is, "I'm too old or too unhealthy." If this proves to be the case, we will often suggest what is called a "second to die" life insurance policy, which means that we are insuring two people—a married couple. The reality is, life insurance is getting cheaper because people are living longer, so from a straight investment standpoint, life insurance is a viable place to keep money. People can qualify for life insurance as they get older, and even if they have some health issues, the insurance company will factor that into their final payment. It makes sense to purchase a plan earlier in life than later, but we have found plans for clients in their eighties.

The cost of life insurance is never as high as people expect, and it always works out relative to the investment a client is putting in. A sixty-six-year old male client in average health will usually pay around $7,500 a year for a $500,000 life insurance policy. We say to this client, "You can take $7,500 a year and give it to your kids and they'll end up spending it on rent or paying off their credit cards. Or you could take that same money, pay for the insurance, and leave them half a million bucks. It's your call." Most clients realize then that insurance isn't a cost, but an investment—clients are investing some money into a product they are guaranteed to get something out of.

At first, seeing that number, $7,500, might startle a client. But to put it in relative terms, let's say a client is 65 and he is going to spend $7,000 a year on life insurance. If he lives twenty years, he has put $140,000 in and will get back $500,000 tax-free. Thinking of these numbers from an investment standpoint, yes, sure, this client could invest that $7,000 in a mutual fund or in some investment strategy, but is he going to be able to put in $7,000 a year, or $140,000 total, and make it worth $500,000 after taxes and fees? No, probably not.

The wealthiest families in the country stopped looking at life insurance as an expense or a payment long ago—they look at it as investment, and that is why their families remain wealthy: they invest in their legacies, and the wealth passes from generation to generation. The wealthiest families finance life insurance cases because they understand the power of tax-free, guaranteed, no-fee returns. They know, as we all do, that they could take a risk and invest their money in the stock market and maybe get lucky, but they also know the value of guaranteed growth—which allows them to go out and spend their money. For our clients who want to leave a legacy, we show them that this is how they leave a legacy on purpose.

The clients who come in saying, "I don't really care about a legacy" often say this because prior to meeting with us, they did not see that it was possible to protect their lifestyles by investing in lifetime income products and then leveraging any excess income through life insurance—to create a legacy on purpose. This is the way the wealthiest people have been doing it for years, and now the average, regular retiree can take that path.

We don't often recommend that our clients take out loans to buy life insurance, but we do take some lessons from the wealthiest families and apply them to our clients' particular situations. What it comes down to is that these lessons are there for our clients' taking, but most of them, prior to meeting us, have been working with brokers who were just trying to invest their money, brokers who never asked them what they wanted their retirement journey to look like.

Once we understand our client's journey, we can build an income plan that will allow them to live the lifestyle they've always wanted in retirement—golf, grandkids, travel, fun—and not ever have to worry about whether the paycheck is going to come next month. We are then going to set up a plan with that income that allows them to give to their kids and to the things they love, and leverage it through life insurance so that when they have passed away, they leave a legacy. Furthermore, we protect all this by purchasing health insurance, both short-term and long-term, proactively diffusing the tax time bomb, and having a plan to deal with inflation.

As we have stated before, the risks of retirement can be compared to the risks of climbing a mountain: you may reach the pinnacle safely and then find yourself unprepared or under-prepared for the journey back to Base Camp. Nobody wants to be there. At the same time, why would anybody want to hoard their money in an IRA, only pull out what the government makes them pull out, and then, after they die and the money goes to their kids, stick those kids with the taxes they will have to pay on it? Wouldn't it be better to use that IRA while living? Similarly, and as we have pointed out before, why live hoping the stock market is going to cooperate? Why resign yourself to a retirement in which every dollar spent could have a negative impact on your future standard of living? With a structured and protected income stream, spending a dollar is a lot less painful. Very few people would say they have worked hard all their lives just to hoard all their money. Most people have worked hard all their lives so that in retirement, they can relax and enjoy their freedom.

Clients come to us with their own unique financial back-grounds and situations, and as we have said throughout this book, some of them have been working with other advisors, planning their retirement. Most people have current life in-surance policies in place, and we review these policies. Most advisors never conduct such reviews, but we make sure our clients have the benefits they think have, and often we find we can maximize those benefits by exchanging them for a newer policy. This is counterintuitive, but much of what we present to our clients is at first surprising—and then it is reassuring. The life insurance audits we conduct sometimes make it possible for our clients to increase their death benefit or decrease or eliminate their premiums. Reducing the monthly payment for their insurance and doubling the total death benefit adds money to their budget, and at the same time increases their legacy without costing them a dime.

So the question, Mr. and Mrs. Jones, is this: Do you want to invest your money and randomly pull it out and hope that you can live the rest of your life the way you've wanted, hoping you don't run out of money, and hoping there will be a little bit of money left over for your kids? Or do you want to create a retirement on purpose, so that your income is structured and sent to you every single month, and you know it is going to be deposited in your account every month, year after year? You're going to be able to take that income and do all the things you've ever wanted to do. You're also going to be able to give more, because the income you're going to have is probably more than what you're going to be able to spend. You're also going to be able to leverage your hard-earned money so that when you pass away, your family will get the amount you want them to get, and they will get it tax-efficiently. We are going to take the clouds of retirement that scare us all (like health care), and we are going to insure against them—using a tool we call *money*. We are going to buy an umbrella so that if it does rain, the rain doesn't harm our lifestyle or our legacy. Which plan do you think makes sense for your retirement?

Because most people don't know there is a path to their ideal retirement other than the one the big firms have been selling, they find themselves running out of money before they run out of life. We know there is another way—a way for our clients to take control and reap all the benefits of the hard work they have done—and leave a legacy for future generations to come.

HOW WE'RE COMPENSATED AND HOW WE CAN CREATE A RICHER RETIREMENT FOR YOU

We ask our clients what they want their retirement journey to look like, and then we create a plan to protect it. Using all the tools in the financial toolbox, we create a plan that includes both safe and risk investment strategies, strategies that provide lifetime income payments that increase over time to keep pace with inflation. We proactively address current and future tax liabilities to make sure clients and their families keep as much of their retirement savings as possible away from Uncle Sam. We also set up a "second to die" life insurance policy to enhance their legacy, so that when they pass away, their family will inherit a guaranteed sum of tax-free money. Finally, we put in place short-term and long-term care policies to protect it all—because, again, even the best plans can be derailed by medical costs that are not taken care of.

Just recently, a client's wife was diagnosed with Alzheimer's. Her care needs will run approximately $75,000 a year. Thankfully, this couple has a long-term care policy in place; if they didn't, they would have had to take the $75,000 from their portfolio, and everything that they had planned for, including their projected standard of living, would now be in jeopardy. But because we put a policy in place, this client's husband and family can get her the care she needs, continue with their lives, and keep all their relationships intact because the total retirement plan is intact. The sense of relief that comes from having a plan in place is priceless.

We strive to create value, and as fee-based investment advisor representatives, we also like to explain to our clients the difference between how they pay us and how they have most likely traditionally paid their advisors. We speak to advisors and consumers in large group settings all across the country, and rarely does either of these groups understand the fees that are paid within a given portfolio. With most of our major life purchases, we would never buy something without understanding the cost, yet we turn over our nest eggs to advisors without having the foggiest idea how, when, why, or what they get paid.

There is no way for consumers to escape fees, but consumers can educate themselves about fees so that they can make better decisions for themselves and their families. There are two basic fees included in every investment decision: a fee for the actual investment and a fee for the advisor. There is a built-in compensation for the advisor, and so as consumers we need to understand how much that is and where it comes from, because when we retire, we will have a cookie jar full of cookies, the bakery will not bake us any more, and we had better understand whose hands are in our cookie jar and how many cookies they're taking.

On the investment side, understand that various fees come out of investments. If you have a mutual fund, for instance, there are annual fees. We have found that many people don't realize that if they hire a brand-name broker to manage that mutual fund, that brand-name broker is charging them a daily fee as well. If they buy a variable annuity, the same thing is happening: a variable annuity includes a deduction of fees from their account for "management" of that particular annuity. Understanding where fees are coming from and whom they are going to helps you to overcome or control fees as you strive to maintain or grow your portfolio throughout retirement.

From the advisor standpoint, we can control the fees for the investments we pick, and that is the very first thing we look at as a firm. We want to recommend quality, solid investments, but we want to make sure that the cost is right, as well. We can control for the second type of fee—the fee that pays us. We get paid by either fees or commissions. The only time we get paid commissions is when we work with an insurance product. When we are involved in any stock market or risk type investment, we are fee-based advisors only. That means our compensation depends on the balances of our clients' accounts—which, as we said before, means that if the client is making money and their accounts are up, we are making more money as well. The opposite is also true—so we have a vested interest in our clients' success. When we say to our clients, "What's happening in your account means just as much to us as it does to you," we are not just blowing smoke as many other advisors do. If we invest our clients' money only to turn around and lose that money, everybody is in trouble. We are in business to be profitable, so we need our clients to also be profitable so we can share in that success.

Conversely, most advisors are commission-based in the stock market, which means that when they sell a client an investment, they get paid up front. If they sell a client a stock or a mutual fund or a bond, the client pays them and the investment goes into their portfolio. People have to ask themselves when their advisor makes a recommendation whether there is an inherent conflict of interest—and there is, because that recommendation comes with compensation. If the client says yes, the advisor gets paid; if the client says no, the advisor doesn't get paid. How should the consumer handle that conflict of interest? When the commission broker tells me I should sell this and buy that, is he saying that because that's what's in my best interest? Or is he saying that because he wants to generate a commission?

In the world of investing, we like to believe these people who are working on commission will not take advantage of us, and certainly not all do. But the reality is that there is only one rule they must follow: they have to do what is *suitable* for the client. They certainly could suggest buying something or selling something that might or might not be in your best interest, but which is certainly *suitable*—and it's the word *suitable* that is tricky. Again, we liken this situation to feeding someone: you could feed someone a candy bar and that's certainly suitable.

You could also feed someone a filet mignon—that's suitable too. But each offering comes with a very different cost structure, nutritional value, and caloric intake. A commission-based broker's only duty is to serve their client something suitable.

When working with fee-based advisors like us, clients don't have to worry about conflicts of interest or the low standard of "suitability." We don't get compensated for transactions, so buying and selling things or readjusting the portfolio later on provides us no compensation. We get paid based on our clients' account balances, so they can be assured that if we give them a recommendation, it's because we feel it is what is in the best interest of their account.

It goes back to the importance of knowing, as a consumer, how your advisor is set up and how they are licensed, so you can understand where their advice is coming from. The rules of a commission-based broker are slanted against the consumer. For a commission-based broker to support himself, he has to continually chase buy-sell transactions. This broker will meet and do business with one client today, but tomorrow he is out chasing the next transaction, and service suffers. By continually focusing on that next transaction, the commission-based broker tends to neglect the management of their existing clients' portfolios. Whereas, because we are fee-based with an ongoing fee, our focus is much more on the management of our current clients' portfolios than it is on chasing transactions. Now, that doesn't mean the commission-based broker is not going to come back to his clients every now and again with recommendations—he will—but now the client has to wonder, again: Is he coming to me now for his benefit, or for mine?

Our clients know we have their benefit in mind, first and foremost. When new clients come to us, they learn right up front about the differences in fees paid on investments and to advisors. Our clients have worked very hard throughout their lives to amass a certain amount of retirement savings, and they value those savings. It is important to them that they protect their savings and protect their lifestyles. Above all, our clients and prospective clients have always had a vision of their retirement, and they come to us saying, "We want you to help us live our vision."

We invite prospective clients to join the ranks of people who do not want their retirement to revolve around CNBC or the Dow Jones, who do not want to spend their days watching the stock market. The people we work with want retirement to be about what they have always thought it would be about—relaxation and fun! Our clients have made good choices throughout their lives, and one of those good choices involved coming to us.

People coming to our office for the first time can expect us to ask, "What is most important to you in your retirement journey? What is important to you in general? What do we need to protect you from? And what do we need to plan for?" New clients are often surprised to find for the very first time that they are working with a team that really cares about them, and not just about their money. We care about what the people we work with are trying to do—we are interested in their hopes and goals. They will hear questions they have probably never heard before, because for us, it isn't simply about what stock or bond our clients should purchase; it is about the clients themselves, and their journey.

Folks who are used to sitting in meetings—or talking on the phone—with a typical advisor, are used to hearing mostly about products. Most advisors are product-driven, and when they meet with new clients for the very first time they say, "Hello. Who are you? How old are you? Okay, this is a good investment and that is a good investment. Goodbye." In our first meeting with a client, he or she immediately senses that our process is outcome-driven—that is, what is the outcome we are trying to achieve with this client, and what investment tools can we use to best ensure this outcome?

If a client wants to reduce his taxes, the brand-name advisor will tell him, "You should buy muni bonds. Muni bonds are tax-free." What the client doesn't realize is that the brand-name advisor is saying that because it is their "sizzle" button: "Boom. Here's tax-free!" We, on the other hand, won't suggest a municipal bond that's tax-free until we look at our client's tax return. We offer no "sizzle, boom" solutions, because it is our practice to look at the client's entire situation first, to figure out whether there are any problems with how they are invested, and whether the way they have been investing has been causing their taxes to be higher than necessary. We will educate our clients on how to achieve the outcomes they desire. Most advisors are only looking for an angle when a client walks through the door, and they try to make the product the answer to retirement. For us, retirement comes down to the entire picture, understanding all the pieces and how they work together to generate the outcome the client is looking for.

Our website, www.citizenadvisory.com, provides our contact information and additional material and news not offered in this book. We encourage everyone to visit our website and get in touch. Wherever you are in the country, we can work with you, or we can refer you to our nationwide network of advisors who are trained in our approach.

We meet with people just like us, people who have worked hard and who have made good choices. We understand them. We know their fears and dreams. Furthermore, because of the expertise and relative experience we have, we sometimes know things about our clients that they might not even know themselves, and when we reveal insight about their retirement for the first time, they begin to see things quite differently. We take the journey with our clients several times a day. We are specialists who provide five-star service, and we are easy to talk to. We look forward to the dialogue our book will inspire.

CPSIA information can be obtained
at www.ICGtesting.com
Printed in the USA
FFOW05n1942010317

9 780692 299807